DESERT WISDOM

SAYINGS FROM THE DESERT FATHERS

Translation and Art by

YUSHI NOMURA

Introduced by

HENRI J. M. NOUWEN

ORBIS BOOKS
Maryknoll, New York 10545

Second printing, December 2001

AN EARLIER VERSION OF THIS WORK WAS PUBLISHED IN 1982 BY DOUBLEDAY & COMPANY.

TRANSLATED FROM TEXTS FOUND IN PATROLOGIA LATINA, VOLUME 73, COMPILED BY J.P. MIGNE, PARIS, 1849, AND IN PATROLOGIA GRAECA, VOLUME 65, COMPILED BY J.P. MIGNE, PARIS, 1858.

DESIGN BY ROBERTA SAVAGE

LIBRARY OF CONGRESS CATALOGING-IN-PUBLICATIONS DATA

DESERT WISDOM: SAYINGS FROM THE DESERT FATHERS/SELECTIONS AND ART BY YUSHI NOMURA; INTRODUCTION BY HENRY J.M. NOUWEN—[REV. ED.]
    P. CM.
    "TRANSLATED FROM TEXTS FOUND IN PATROLOGIA LATINA, VOLUME 73, COMPILED BY J.P. MIGNE, PARIS, 1849, AND IN PATROLOGIA GRAECA, VOLUME 65, COMPILED BY J.P. MIGNE, PARIS, 1858"—T.P. VERSO
    ISBN 1-57075-371-7 (PBK.)
    DESERT FATHERS—QUOTATIONS. 2. SPIRITUAL LIFE—CHRISTIANITY— QUOTATIONS, MAXIMS, ETC. 3. MONASTIC AND RELIGIOUS LIFE—QUOTATIONS, MAXIMS, ETC. I. NOMURA, YUSHI

BR63 .D47 2001
270.2—DC21   2001018524

For my late father, a son of the Samurai,
from whom I inherited a sense of tradition,
and for my late mother,
whose way of life led me to the Christian faith.

CONTENTS

PREFACE

These stories and sayings of the Christian hermits from fourth- and fifth-century Egypt have a unique place in Christian tradition. They have been a source of inspiration to the Western monastic movement throughout its history and are considered by scholars to be one of the important groups of documents among early Christian writings. Yet to others they are not well known today. As an effort to convey their richness and uniqueness to a wider group, I selected and translated these stories from the Latin and Greek texts, and visually interpreted them with Japanese brush and ink.

For this translation I used texts found in *Patrologia Latina*, volume 73, compiled by J.P. Migne, Paris, 1849, and in *Patrologia Graeca*, volume 65, compiled by J.P. Migne, Paris, 1858. I have tried to retain the simple, down-to-earth quality of the texts by translating them into plain modern English and have used gender-inclusive language wherever possible. I believe that the spirit of these stories is inclusive even where the language is not and so have used the drawings themselves to illustrate this. I kept the Aramaic words "Abba" and "Amma" in this translation. They mean "Father" and "Mother" and were widely used to address spiritual fathers and mothers with love and respect.

This project had its beginning in a course on Desert Spirituality and Contemporary Ministry at Yale Divinity School, which was taught by Henri J.M. Nouwen. Yet Henri's understanding and encouragement has far exceeded the classroom. If I had not had such overwhelming support, spiritual and otherwise, from this wonderful teacher and great friend, it would have been utterly impossible for this book to take its present form. Karin Johnson not only helped me to correct and refine my English style, but also painstakingly checked the translation against the original Latin and Greek texts and gave me many important suggestions. Through her loving personality Karin has given me a sense of assurance in the course of this work. There are numerous people involved, directly and indirectly, in the various stages of this project. Particularly, my dear friends at Yale Divinity School, the soup kitchen in New Haven, and the Church of the Living Hope in East Harlem, New York City, have been my sources of encouragement and inspiration from the beginning. Finally, I would like to thank my late father and sister for their understanding of this project, which kept me far from home.

Yushi Nomura

INTRODUCTION

This is a book with stories from the desert. They are translated and decorated by my friend Yushi Nomura. I am grateful for the opportunity to introduce this splendid book because from the moment the plans for this project were first expressed, I have felt very closely connected with their realization.

In this introduction I want to do three things. First of all, I want to describe the remarkable way in which these desert stories bridged the distance between Japan, the United States, Holland, and Peru and linked me in a very personal way to Yushi and his work. Second, I would like to present the desert fathers and desert mothers and show how their spiritual struggle and ours are essentially the same. Finally, I hope to convince you, who will read these stories, that they have the power to offer not just new insights, but even new life.

I am writing these words in Pamplona Alta, a huge barrio at the outskirts of Lima, Peru. Twenty-five years ago this was a raw empty desert. Today this desert has been converted into a city where more than one hundred thousand poor Peruvians try to survive.

I have been here only four weeks, but these four weeks seem ages away from Holland, where I was born, spent an easy youth, became a priest, studied, and taught; ages away, too, from Connecticut in the United States, where I lived and worked with theology students during the last ten years.

What am I doing here in this hot, dusty, desert city? What am I doing in this strange new world with countless little kids running up to me, hugging and kissing me, and using me as a climbing tree; with numerous teenagers playing soccer in the loose yellow sand; with many friendly men and women saying "Buenos días"; and with an occasional drunkard putting his arm around me and raising a profound question about the meaning of life? What am I doing in this treeless place, with loudspeakers shouting local news over the housetops, with squeaking phonographs playing until the early hours of the morning, with thousands of underfed, barking dogs and crowing cocks, with vendors and crying babies, with many curses and tears, and with endless dark fears about the future of it all? Why am I here so far from books, students, discussion groups, and lecture halls? I do not have a precise answer, but I do know that voices from another desert have a lot to do with it. They are the voices of the old Egyptian hermits of the fourth and fifth centuries. Ever since I heard their stories and read their sayings, I knew that there was a wisdom, hidden from the learned and revealed to mere children, worth searching for.

One of these desert fathers was Arsenius, a wealthy, well-educated aristocrat who had left Rome to find his salvation in the desert. Of him the story goes: "One day Abba Arsenius was asking an old Egyptian man for advice about what he was thinking. There was someone who saw this and said to him: 'Abba Arsenius, why is a person like you, who has such a great knowledge of Greek and Latin, asking a peasant like this about your thoughts?' He replied: 'Indeed, I have learned the knowledge of Latin and Greek, yet I have not learned even the alphabet of this peasant.'"

Maybe this is why I am here. To learn a new alphabet from Pablo, Sofía, Pablito, Juanito, and María, the family with whom I live. It is an alphabet that spells patience, humility, joy, hope, and love in a wholly new way: the way of the poor, the way of the victims of oppression and exploitation, the way of the God who became a servant.

While I am finding the desert wisdom in Peru, my friend Yushi Nomura is finding it among the poor in the soup kitchen of New Haven, Connecticut. And to him, too, the Abbas and Ammas from the Egyptian desert are giving answers to his question, "Why am I here?" Yushi came from Japan to the United States to study. When he came across the simple but profound stories from the Egyptian desert, his Japanese spirit was so deeply moved that he wanted to write them down in a way that they could be not only read, but also seen and felt. And thus, with his sensitive mind and artistic hand, he drew these ancient words anew so that they would touch more directly the human heart. Yushi knew that letters can do more than convey an idea. The Japanese calligraphers had shown him that carefully drawn letters are themselves a message and can reach deeper into the soul than their meaning alone. Yushi also knew that the Christian monk in Egypt and the Buddhist monk in Japan are not strangers to each other. Both struggle to leave behind the illusions and deceptions of this world and both search for the undying light of God. Therefore Yushi placed the desert stories from Egypt in the monastic milieu of Japan, and so he created a place in which the Buddha and the Christ in him could reach out to each other.

While working in this way, the wisdom of the desert became flesh for him in the poor people of New Haven. In a letter to me in Peru he says: "At the soup kitchen I see more and more jobless people coming by, some taking their children with them. I always love to eat with them, listening to their stories, sharing what I know. They are my friends, teachers, and cheerleaders. And I want to be to them at least as much as they have been to me. When I am talking with them, the Abbas and Ammas from the Egyptian desert come to my heart and tell me what to say. At other times, I see 'Abba and Amma quality' in my friends at the soup kitchen. And that makes me feel as though I were a little brother surrounded by the community of desert fathers and mothers." These wonderful words make me aware how small the distance between Lima and New Haven really is.

Yushi and I met in a classroom of the Yale Divinity School. I spoke about the desert fathers and desert mothers. He listened and took notes. But then it happened that the desert stories started to do their mysterious work of conversion. With his calligraphy and drawings he helped me see more than I had shown him. He became my teacher by making me look at these stories as if I had never seen them before. To us happened what happened in that faraway Egyptian desert many centuries ago: "There was an old man who had a good disciple. One day he was annoyed and drove the disciple out. Yet the disciple sat down outside the cell and waited. When the old man opened the door, he found him sitting there, and repented before him, saying: 'You are my father, for your humility and patience have overcome my narrow-mindedness. Come inside! From now on, you are the old man and the father, for sure, and I am the young one and the disciple. For your good works have surpassed my old age.'"

Holland, Peru, Japan, and the United States seem such different worlds, so far apart not only in miles but also in thinking, feeling, and acting. But when Yushi and I came to see our new surroundings through the eyes of the Abbas and Ammas of the desert, we found a unity between us that transcends all distances and all differences, a spiritual unity that cannot be undone by any human-made boundaries.

Thus this book not only contains many stories, but also has its own story, a story of friendship made possible by the divine love reflected to both of us in the wisdom of the desert.

Who were these desert fathers and desert mothers? They were men and women who withdrew themselves from the compulsions and manipulations of their power-hungry society in order to fight the demons and to encounter the God of love in the desert. They were people who had become keenly aware that after the period of persecutions and acceptance of Christianity as a "normal" part of society, the radical call of Christ to leave father, mother, brother, and sister, to take up the cross and follow him, had been watered down to an acceptable and comfortable religiosity and had lost its converting power. The Abbas and Ammas of the Egyptian desert had left this world of compromise, adaptation, and a lukewarm spirituality and had chosen solitude, silence, and prayer as the new way to be living witnesses of the crucified and risen Lord. Thus they became the new "martyrs," witnessing not with their blood, but with their single-minded dedication to a humble life of manual work, fasting, and prayer.

The life of these ancient hermits can be seen as a hard and often painful struggle to find their true identity. The world they tried to escape is the world in which money, power, fame, success, influence, and good connections are the ways to self-esteem. It is the world that says, "You are what you have." This false identity never gives the security and safety which we are searching for, but throws us in the spiral of a permanent desire for more—more money, more power, more friends—in the illusion that one day we will arrive at that dreamplace where nobody and nothing can harm us. The hermits of the desert were deeply conscious of the fact that not only the society but also the church had been corrupted by this illusion. They escaped into the desert to free themselves from this compulsive self, to shake off the many layers of self-deception and reclaim their true self. In the desert, away from human praise and criticism, they could slowly grow into the knowledge that they are not who people say they are, but who God made them to be: His own sons and daughters, created and recreated in His Spirit. In the desert they came to the realization that as long as they kept trying to find their identity outside of God, they ended up in that vicious spiral of wanting more and more. But there they also discovered that their true identity is securely planted in the first love of God Himself and that this first love frees them from their fearful compulsions and allows them to relate to their own society freely, joyfully, and peacefully.

The way of life of the Abbas and Ammas of the desert makes it clear that finding our true identity is not the simple result of having a new insight. Reclaiming our true self requires a total transformation. It requires a long and often slow process in which we enter more and more into the truth, that is, into a true relationship with God and, through Him, with ourselves.

The desert—the Egyptian desert of the Abbas and Ammas, but also our own spiritual desert—has a double quality: it is wilderness and paradise. It is wilderness, because in the desert we struggle against the "wild beasts" that attack us, the demons of boredom, sadness, anger, and pride. However, it is also paradise, because there we can meet God and taste already His peace and joy. Amma Syncletica said: "In the beginning, there is struggle and a lot of work for those who come near to God. But after that, there is indescribable joy. It is just like building a fire: At first it's smoky and your eyes water, but later you get the desired result. Thus we ought to light the divine fire in ourselves with tears and effort."

It would, however, be a mistake to think that the desert fathers and desert mothers only went to the desert for their own salvation. This was certainly an important aspect of their monastic life, but it was never disconnected from a deep sense of service to the larger Christian community. Their struggle was not just for themselves but also for their fellow Christians. They considered the desert as the place to which the demons withdrew after their destructive work in the cities and towns. They went to the desert to enter into a direct and unambiguous combat with these demons, a combat in the name of the whole church. The hermits of the desert were hermits for others. Thus it is easy to understand that many people from the cities and towns, laypeople, priests, and bishops came to visit them and ask for their advice, for guidance, or just for a word of comfort. It is also quite understandable that they themselves always considered it as their primary obligation to be hospitable to their visitors, and to help the poor and needy. Even the most severe form of asceticism was considered less important than service to the neighbor. That is why one of the wise men of the desert says: "Even if the brother who fasts six days were to hang himself by the nose, he could not equal the one who serves the sick."

Escaping the world was, therefore, for the desert fathers and mothers like escaping from a prison with the intention to liberate the other prisoners too.

From the many desert stories, Yushi Nomura has made a careful selection. The stories he presents in this book are stories that can speak directly to us, who live at least fifteen centuries after they were first written down. They do not require much explanation. What they do require is a spirit of discipleship, that is, a willingness to listen, to learn, and to be converted. They all touch our own spiritual concerns. They respond to our disturbing feelings of anger and our undesirable desires for pleasure and revenge. They point to humility and a nonjudgmental way of life. They compare words with works, speaking with silence, and prayer with thoughts. They offer concrete suggestions about the best way to be a teacher and about how to relate to human rules. They stress the importance of service to the neighbor and they show the fruits of obedience, prayer, and simple trust in God. Undergirding all these concrete hints, suggestions, and counsels is the constant reminder of God's loving and merciful presence in our lives.

During the months in which Yushi was translating these stories from Greek and Latin into the English language, writing them down in beautiful letters and decorating them with Japanese drawings, he wrote me: "These stories have such power that I am able to relate the spirit of the desert to the spirit of the people I meet. These stories have their strength in their short, direct, honest, and simple forms, which came out of the actual life experiences of those brothers and sisters. They are neither legends nor parables, but they are life-giving stories. I am always struck by their power as I stand somewhere between the stories and my friends." This observation, which comes forth from Yushi's own intimate life with these stories, is probably their best introduction, because in these words Yushi captures precisely the reason why we should read them: They are life-giving stories.

The desert fathers and mothers did not offer theories on the spiritual life, they did not give lectures or write essays. They were simple hermits who lived their lives silently, away from the great economic and cultural centers of their day, earning their living with manual work and praying unceasingly. The words we have from them are responses to their fellow hermits, to their disciples, and to their occasional visitors. They are concrete answers to concrete questions. They were never meant to be general truths. They were meant to help a searching brother or sister, to correct an erring fellow monk, to give courage to a despairing friend, or to console a saddened parent.

Paradoxically, however, these sayings which were meant for just one human being have the power to give life to many. They share that power with many Zen and Hasidic sayings. What is most personal, most concrete, and most specific is able to touch the hearts of people living in very different places, in very different times, and in very different circumstances. In their uniqueness they create a large space in which many can find a home. There is realism, humor, irony, reproach, invitation, challenge, and fervent zeal. Together these qualities form the safe and flexible boundaries within which we can move and listen to God's call for us.

One monk who asked his Abba how to live his life received the words: "Rejoice always, pray constantly, and in all circumstances give thanks." Another monk, raising the same question, heard the answer: "Do not be confident in your own righteousness, do not worry about a thing once it's done, and control your tongue and your stomach." And we, who read these divergent responses, smile and realize not only that these two monks must have been quite different, but also that there is space in our own hearts for both of them. Thus the stories from the desert become stories for all of us who seek God with a sincere heart.

To you, who pick up this book and let these sayings enter deeply into your innermost being, Yushi and I want to say that this book is a work of love, the fruit of a deep friendship and a way of whispering into your ears what Abba Bessarion whispered into the ears of Abba Doulas: "God is here, and God is everywhere."

Henri J. M. Nouwen
Peru, 1982

DESERT WISDOM

*A*bba Poemen said about Abba Pior that every single day he made a fresh beginning.

*A*bba Isaiah said: When someone wishes to render evil for evil, he is able to hurt his brother's conscience even by a single nod.

A bba Sisoes said: Seek God, and not where God lives.

3

*O*ne of the fathers said: Just as it is impossible to see your face in troubled water, so also the soul, unless it is clear of alien thoughts, is not able to pray to God in contemplation.

It was said about Abba Agathon that for three years he carried a pebble around in his mouth until he learned to be silent.

*A*bba John the Little said: We have abandoned a light burden, namely self-criticism, and taken up a heavy burden, namely self-justification.

*A*bba John of Thebaid said: Above all things, a monk ought to be humble. In fact, this is the first commandment of the Savior who said: Blessed are the poor in spirit, for theirs is the kingdom of heaven.

Once the rule was made in Scetis that they should fast for the entire week before Easter. During this week, however, some brothers came from Egypt to see Abba Moses, and he made a modest meal for them. Seeing the smoke, the neighbors said to the priests of the church of that place: Look, Moses has broken the rule and is cooking food at his place. Then the priests said: When he comes out, we will talk to him. When the Sabbath came, the priests, who knew Abba Moses' great way of life, said to him in public: Oh, Abba Moses, you did break the commandment made by people, but you have firmly kept the commandment of God.

bba Isaiah said to those beginners who were off to a good start, obedient to the tradition of the holy fathers: Take for instance purple cloth: the original dye cannot be removed. And: Just as the young branches can easily be corrected and bent, so can beginners who are obedient.

*A*bba Mios was asked by a soldier whether God would forgive a sinner. After instructing him at some length, the old man asked him: Tell me, my dear, if your cloak were torn, would you throw it away? Oh, no! he replied, I would mend it and wear it again. The old man said to him: Well, if you care for your cloak, will not God show mercy to his own creature?

It was said about John the Little that one day he said to his older brother: I want to be free from care and not to work but to worship God without interruption. And he took his robe off, and went into the desert. After staying there one week, he returned to his brother. And when he knocked at the door, his brother asked without opening it: Who is it? He replied: It's John, your brother.

The brother said: John has become an angel and is not among people anymore. Then he begged and said: It's me! But his brother did not open the door and left him there in distress until the next morning. And he finally opened the door and said: If you are a human being, you have to work again in order to live. Then John repented, saying: Forgive me, brother, for I was wrong.

In Scetis, a brother went to see Abba
Moses and begged him for a word. And
the old man said: Go and sit in your cell, and
your cell will teach you everything.

$\mathcal{A}$bba Anthony said: The time is coming when people will be insane, and when they see someone who is not insane, they will attack that person saying: You are insane because you are not like us.

*A*bba Isaac said: Abba Pambo used to say that the monk's coat should be such that even if he threw it out of the cell and left it for three days, still nobody would take it.

Some old men came to see Abba Poemen, and said to him: Tell us, when we see brothers dozing during the sacred office, should we pinch them so they will stay awake? The old man said to them: Actually, if I saw a brother sleeping, I would put his head on my knees and let him rest.

*A*bba Evagrius said that there was a brother, called Serapion, who didn't own anything except the Gospel, and this he sold to feed the poor. And he said these words, which are worth remembering: I have even sold the very word which commanded me: Sell everything, and give to the poor.

*A*mma Syncletica said: If you happen to live in a community, do not move to another place, for it will harm you greatly. If a bird leaves her eggs, they never hatch. So also the monk and the nun grow cold and dead in faith by going from place to place.

One day Abba Macarius was on his way
back to his cell from the marsh, carrying palm leaves. And look! There was the
devil on the road, holding a sickle and trying
to attack him. But he couldn't, and said: I am
suffering a great deal of violence from you,
O Macarius. I do everything you do for sure.

When you fast, I do not eat, and when you keep vigil, I don't go to sleep at all. Yet there is only one thing in which you outdo me. Then Abba Macarius asked: What is it? The devil replied: It is your humility, and because of it I am powerless against you.

*A*bba Silvanus said: Woe to the person whose reputation is greater than his work.

*O*ne day Abba Arsenius was asking an old Egyptian man for advice about what he was thinking. There was someone who saw this and said to him: Abba Arsenius, why is a person like you, who has such a great knowledge of Greek and Latin, asking a peasant like this about your thoughts? He replied: Indeed, I have learned the knowledge of Latin and Greek, yet I have not learned even the alphabet of this peasant.

A brother who was living among other brothers asked Abba Bessarion: What should I do? The old man replied: Be silent, and do not measure yourself against the others.

There was a man who was leading an ascetic life and not eating bread. He went to visit an old man. It happened that pilgrims also dropped by, and the old man fixed a modest meal for them. When they sat together to eat, the brother who was fasting picked up a single soaked pea and chewed it. When they arose from the table, the old man took the brother aside and said: Brother, when you go to visit somewhere, do not display your way of life, but if you want to keep to it, stay in your cell and never come out. He accepted what the old man said, and after that behaved like the others whenever he met with them.

*A*mma Syncletica said: In the beginning, there is struggle and a lot of work for those who come near to God. But after that, there is indescribable joy. It is just like building a fire: At first it's smoky and your eyes water, but later you get the desired result. Thus we ought to light the divine fire in ourselves with tears and effort.

It was said about one brother that when he had woven baskets and put handles on them, he heard a monk next door saying: What shall I do? The trader is coming but I don't have handles to put on my baskets! Then he took the handles off his own baskets and brought them to his neighbor, saying: Look, I have these left over. Why don't you put them on your baskets? And he made his brother's work complete, as there was need, leaving his own unfinished.

A brother came to see Abba Theodore, and started to talk and inquire about things that he himself had not tried yet. The old man said to him: You have not found a boat, or put your gear into it, and you haven't even sailed, but you seem to have arrived in the city already! Well, do your work first; then you will come to the point you are talking about now.

It was said about Abba John
the Little that he went away
to an old Theban in Scetis who
lived in the desert. Once his Abba
took a piece of dry wood, planted
it, and said to him: Water it every
day with a bottle of water until it
bears fruit. The water, however,
was so far away from there that
John had to go out late in the
evening and come back the next
morning. Three years later, the
tree came to life and bore fruit.
Then the old man took some of
the fruit and brought it to the
church, and said to the brothers:
Take and eat the fruit of obedience!

An old man said: I never wanted work that was useful to me but loss to my brother. For I have this expectation, that what helps my brother is fruitful for me.

*A*n old man said: Constant prayer quickly straightens out our thoughts.

A brother asked an old man:
What shall I do? For many thoughts
are bothering me, and I don't know how to
fight back. The old man said: Do not fight
against all of them, but against one. In fact,
all thoughts of monks have a single head.
Therefore, you have to figure out which and
what kind it is, and fight against it. By doing
so, you can defeat the rest of those thoughts.

A brother who had sinned was
expelled by the priest from the
church. But Abba Bessarion stood up and
went out with him, saying: I too am a sinner.

The old men used to say: If you see a young person climbing up to heaven by his own will, hold him by the foot, and pull him down to the ground, for it is just not good for him.

One day, when Abba Agathon was on his way to town to sell small utensils, he saw a leper sitting on the roadside, who asked: Where are you going? Abba Agathon replied: To town, to sell these things. Then he said: Do me a favor, and take me there. So he carried him to the town. Then he said: Put me down wherever you sell those things. So he did. And when he sold one item, the leper asked: How much did you sell it for? So he told him how much it was. Then he said: Buy me something nice. So he bought it. He sold another item.

Then the leper asked: And how much was it?
So he told him the price. Then he said: Buy
me this. So he bought it. After selling everything, he wanted to go. Then the leper asked:
Are you going back? He replied: Sure. Then
he said: Do me a favor again and take me
back to the place where you found me. So he
carried him back to the place where he was.
Then he said: You are blessed, Agathon, by
the Lord, in heaven and on earth! As the
Abba lifted his eyes, he saw nobody, for it
was an angel of the Lord who had come to
test him.

*A*bba Hyperichius said: The person who teaches others by actions, not by words, is truly wise.

A brother asked Abba Hieracus: Give me a word. How can I be saved? The old man said to him: Sit in your cell; if you are hungry, eat; if you are thirsty, drink; and just do not speak evil of anyone, and you will be saved.

*A*n old man said: If you have words, but no work, you are like a tree with leaves but no fruit. But just as a tree bearing fruit is also leafy, a person who has good work comes up with good words.

*A*bba Zeno, the disciple of Abba Silvanus, said: Never live in a well-known place, nor stay with a famous person, nor lay a foundation on which you are going to build a cell someday.

A brother came to visit Abba Silvanus at Mount Sinai. When he saw the brothers working hard, he said to the old man: Do not work for the food that perishes. For Mary has chosen the good part. Then the old man called his disciple: Zachary, give this brother a book and put him in an empty cell. Now, when it was three o'clock, the brother kept looking out the door, to see whether someone would come to call him for the meal. But nobody called him, so he got up, went to see the old man, and asked: Abba,

didn't the brothers eat today? The old man
said: Of course we did. Then he said: Why
didn't you call me? The old man replied: You
are a spiritual person and do not need that
kind of food, but since we are earthly, we
want to eat, and that's why we work. Indeed,
you have chosen the good part, reading all day
long, and not wanting to eat earthly food.
When the brother heard this, he repented and
said: Forgive me, Abba. Then the old man said
to him: Mary certainly needed Martha, and it
is really by Martha's help that Mary is praised.

Saint Syncletica said: Just as a treasure exposed is quickly spent, so also any virtue that becomes famous or well publicized vanishes. Just as wax is quickly melted by fire, so the soul is emptied by praise, and loses firmness of virtue.

 44

*A*bba Poemen said to Abba Joseph: Tell me how I can become a monk. And he replied: If you want to find rest here and hereafter, say in every occasion, Who am I? and do not judge anyone.

bba John the Little said: No one can build a house from the top down; rather, you build the foundation first and then build upwards. People said to him: What do you mean by that? He said to them: The foundation means your neighbor whom you must win, and you ought to start from there. For all the commandments of Christ depend on this.

*A*n old man said: If you have lost gold or silver, you can find something in place of what you lost. However, if you lose time you cannot replace what you lost.

*O*nce a brother committed a sin in Scetis, and the elders assembled and sent for Abba Moses. He, however, did not want to go. Then the priest sent a message to him, saying: Come, everybody is waiting for you. So he finally got up to go. And he took a worn-out basket with holes, filled it with sand, and carried it along.

The people who came to meet him said: What is this, Father? Then the old man said: My sins are running out behind me, yet I do not see them. And today I have come to judge the sins of someone else. When they heard this, they said nothing to the brother, and pardoned him.

A brother asked Abba Poemen: What does it mean to get angry at one's brother without cause? And he replied: When your brother attacks you, whatever the insults are, if you get angry at him, you are getting angry without cause. Even if he were to pull out your right eye, and to cut off your right hand, if you get angry at him, you are getting angry without cause. Yet if he were to try to take you away from God, then get angry!

 50

*A*bba Poemen asked Abba Anthony: What should I do? The old man said: Do not be confident in your own righteousness, do not worry about a thing once it's done, and control your tongue and your stomach.

A brother asked Abba Pambo: Why do the spirits hold me back from doing good to my neighbor? The old man said: Do not talk like that, or you will make God a liar. Why don't you say, I don't want to be kind at all? Long ago, God indeed said: I have given you the power to tread upon scorpions and serpents, and over all the strength of the Enemy. Now why don't you stamp down the evil spirit?

A brother who was insulted by another brother came to Abba Sisoes, and said to him: I was hurt by my brother, and I want to avenge myself. The old man tried to console him and said: Don't do that, my child. Rather leave vengeance to God. But he said: I will not quit until I avenge myself. Then the old man said: Let us pray, brother; and standing up, he said: O God, we no longer need you to take care of us since we now avenge ourselves. Hearing these words, the brother fell at the feet of the old man and said: I am not going to fight with my brother any more. Forgive me, Abba.

*O*nce two brothers went to visit an old man. It was not the old man's habit, however, to eat every day. When he saw the brothers, he welcomed them with joy, and said: Fasting has its own reward, but if you eat for the sake of love you satisfy two commandments, for you give up your own will and also fulfill the commandment to refresh others.

Abba Nisteros the Great was walking through the desert with a brother, and seeing a dragon, they ran away. Then the brother said to him: Are you afraid too, Father? The old man replied: I was not afraid, my son, but it was good for me to run away from the dragon; otherwise, I would not have escaped from the spirit of vainglory.

It was said about an old man that he
endured seventy weeks of fasting, eating
only once a week. He asked God about certain
words in the Holy Scripture, but God did not
answer him. Then he said to himself: Look, I
have put in this much effort, but I haven't
made any progress. So now I will go to see my
brother, and ask him. And when he had gone

out, closed the door and started off, an angel of the Lord was sent to him, and said: Seventy weeks of fasting have not brought you near to God. But now that you are humbled enough to go to your brother, I have been sent to you to reveal the meaning of the words. Then the angel explained the meaning that the old man was seeking, and went away.

$\mathcal{A}$bba Poemen said: Teach your mouth to speak what is in your heart.

*A*bba Poemen said:
The nature of water
is yielding, and that of a
stone is hard. Yet if you
hang a bottle filled with
water above the stone so
that the water drips drop by
drop, it will wear a hole in
the stone. In the same way
the word of God is tender,
and our heart is hard. So
when people hear the word
of God frequently, their
hearts are opened to the
fear of God.

*A*bba Elias said: Unless the mind sings with the body, the labor is in vain. And: Whoever loves tribulation will have joy and refreshment afterwards.

There was an old man who had a good disciple. One day he was annoyed and drove the disciple out. Yet the disciple sat down outside of the cell and waited. When the old man opened the door, he found him sitting there, and repented before him, saying: You are my father, for your humility and patience have overcome my narrow-mindedness. Come inside! From now on, you are the old man and the father, for sure, and I am the young one and the disciple. For your good works have surpassed my old age.

When Abba Macarius was in Egypt, he found a man with a mule stealing his belongings. Then, as though he were a stranger, he helped the robber to load the animal, and peacefully sent him off, saying:

We have brought nothing into the world, and
we cannot take anything with us. The Lord
has given, and as he has wished, so it has
happened. Blessed be the Lord in all things.

Once some bandits came to the hermitage of an old man, and said: We have come to take away everything in your cell. And he said: Whatever you see, my sons. Then they took whatever they found in the cell and went away. But they left behind a little bag that was out of sight. But the old man picked it up, and ran after them, shouting: My sons, take this! You forgot it! They were indeed amazed by the endurance of the old man, and brought everything back into the cell. And all of them repented and said to each other: He really is a man of God.

The devil appeared to a brother, in the disguise of an angel of light, and said to him: I am the angel Gabriel and I have been sent to you. However, the brother said to him: See if you are not being sent to someone else. I certainly do not deserve to have an angel sent to me. Immediately, the devil disappeared.

*A*brother said to an old man: There are two brothers. One of them stays quietly in his cell, fasting for six days at a time, and imposing on himself a good deal of discipline, and the other serves the sick.

Which one of them is more acceptable to God? The old man replied: Even if the brother who fasts six days were to hang himself by the nose, he could not equal the one who serves the sick.

*A*bba Xanthias said: A dog is better than I am because it also has love, but it does not pass judgment.

A philosopher asked Saint Anthony: Father, how can you be enthusiastic when the comfort of books has been taken away from you? He replied: My book, O Philosopher, is the nature of created things, and whenever I want to read the Word of God, it is usually right in front of me.

There were two old men who had lived together for many years, and they never quarreled. Now one of them said: Let us try to quarrel once just like other people do. And the other replied: I don't know how a quarrel happens. Then the first said: Look, I put a brick between us, and I say, This is mine, and you say, No, it's mine, and after that a quarrel begins. So they placed a brick between them, and one of them said: This is mine, and the other said: No, it's mine. And he replied: Indeed, it's all yours, so take it away with you! And they went away unable to fight with each other.

*O*ne old man went to visit another. As they were talking, one of them said: I am dead to this world. The other man said to him: Do not be so sure about yourself until you are really dead, for you may say that you are dead, yet Satan is not dead.

A leader of a community asked Abba
Poemen: How can I gain the fear of
God? Abba Poemen replied: How indeed
can we gain the fear of God when we have
bellies full of cheese and jars of salted fish?

A noble man whom nobody knew
came to Scetis carrying gold with
him, and asked the priest of the desert to
distribute it to the brothers. The priest said
to him: The brothers do not need it. But he
was very insistent and was not satisfied, so
he put the whole sum in a basket at the
entrance of the church. And the priest said:
Whoever needs it may take some. But
nobody touched it or even looked at it. Then
the old man said: God has accepted your
offering. Go, and give it to the poor. And the
man went away greatly benefited.

*A*bba Sarmatas said: I prefer a person who has sinned if he knows that he sinned and has repented, over a person who has not sinned and considers himself to be righteous.

*A*bba Doulas, the disciple of Abba Bessarion, said: When we were walking along the sea one day, I was thirsty, so I said to Abba Bessarion, Abba, I am very thirsty. Then the old man prayed, and said to me, Drink from the sea. The water was sweet when I drank it. And I poured it into a flask, so that I would not be thirsty later. Seeing this, the old man asked me, Why are you doing that? I answered, Excuse me, but it's so that I won't be thirsty later on. Then the old man said, God is here, and God is everywhere.

One day, Theophilus of holy memory, the bishop of Alexandria, came to Scetis. And the brothers who gathered said to Abba Pambo: Say a word to the bishop so that his soul may be benefited here. The old man replied: If he is not inspired by my silence, he will not be inspired by my words either.

*A*bba Poemen said: If a monk overcomes two things, he can be free from this world. And a brother asked: What are they? He replied: Bodily ease and vainglory.

A brother came to Abba Poemen and said: Abba, a variety of thoughts are coming into my mind and I am in danger. The old man took him out in the air and said: Open your robe and take hold of the wind. And he answered: No, I cannot do it. The old man said: If you cannot do it, neither can you prevent those thoughts from coming in. But what you should do is to stand firm against them.

There was a man in Egypt whose son was paralyzed, and he brought him to the cell of blessed Macarius, and left him crying at the door, and went away. Then the old man looked around, and saw the boy crying, and said to him: Who brought you here? And he said: My father abandoned me here and left. And the old man said: Stand up and go get him! The boy was healed at once, and went to find his father, and thus they went home together.

Once some people came to an old man in Thebaid, bringing a person possessed by a demon, hoping that he might be cured by the old man. Being asked persistently for quite some time, the old man finally said to the demon: Go out of God's creation. And the demon replied: I will go out, but let me ask

you just one thing. Tell me, who are the goats
and who are the sheep? Then the old man
said: A goat is someone such as I am, but as
for the sheep, well, only God knows. Hearing
this the demon cried out in a loud voice:
Look, because of your humility I am going
out! And he went away that very moment.

*A*bba Isidore of Pelusia said: Living without speaking is better than speaking without living. For a person who lives rightly helps us by silence, while one who talks too much merely annoys us. If, however, words and life go hand in hand, it is the perfection of all philosophy.

*A*bba Poemen said: There is one sort of person who seems to be silent, but inwardly criticizes other people. Such a person is really talking all the time. Another may talk from morning till night, but says only what is meaningful, and so keeps silence.

*A*mma Syncletica said: It is good not to get angry. But if it should happen, do not allow your day to go by affected by it. For it is said: Do not let the sun go down. Otherwise, the rest of your life may be affected by it. Why hate a person who hurts you, for it is not that person who is unjust, but the devil. Hate the sickness, but not the sick person.

Abba Joseph asked Abba Poemen: How should we fast? And Abba Poemen said: I myself think it's good to eat every day, a little at a time, so as not to get full. Abba Joseph said: Well, when you were young, didn't you used to fast for two days at a time? And the old man said: Believe me, indeed I did, for three days, and even a week. But the great elders tried all of this, and found that it is good to eat every day, a little less each time. In this way, they showed us the royal highway, for it is light and easy.

One day, Abba Isaac the Theban went to a monastic community and he saw a brother doing wrong, and he condemned him. As he returned to the desert, an angel of the Lord came and stood in front of the door of his cell and said: I won't let you in. He asked: What's the matter? And the angel

replied: God has sent me to ask you where
he should cast the sinner on whom you
passed judgment. Immediately he repented
and said: I was wrong. Forgive me. And the
angel said: Get up, God has forgiven you. In
the future be sure not to judge someone
before God passes judgment.

Amma Theodora said: A teacher ought to be a stranger to love of domination, and a foreigner to vainglory, far from arrogance, neither deceived by flattery, nor blinded by gifts, nor a slave to the stomach, nor held back by anger, but rather should be patient, kind, and as far as possible humble. He ought to be self-disciplined, tolerant, diligent, and a lover of souls.

A brother asked an old man: What is humility? And the old man said: To do good to those who hurt you. The brother said: If you cannot go that far, what should you do? The old man replied: Get away from them and keep your mouth shut.

*A*bba Or said: Either flee from people, or laugh at the world and the people in it, and make a fool of yourself in many things.

bba Lot went to see Abba Joseph and said: Abba, as much as I am able I practice a small rule, a little fasting, some prayer and meditation, and remain quiet, and as much as possible I keep my thoughts clean. What else should I do? Then the old man stood up and stretched out his hands toward heaven, and his fingers became like ten torches of flame. And he said: If you wish, you can become all flame.

*A*mma Sarah said: If I pray to God that all people might be inspired because of me, I would find myself repenting at the door of every house. I would rather pray that my heart be pure toward everybody.

*A*bba Nilus said: Whatever you do in revenge against your brother who has hurt you will appear all at once in your heart at the time of prayer.

 94

The old men used to say: When we are tested, we are more humbled, for God knows our weakness and protects us. Yet when we boast, God takes his protection away from us. Then we are really lost.

As he was dying, Abba Benjamin taught his sons this: Do this, and you'll be saved: Rejoice always, pray constantly, and in all circumstances give thanks.

97

A bba Euprepios said: Bodily things
consist of matter. The person who
loves worldly things loves stumbling blocks.
When we lose something, therefore, we
should accept it with joy and thanks, as we
have been relieved from care.

Abba Sisoes the Theban said to his disciple: Tell me what you see in me and in turn I will tell you what I see in you. His disciple said to him: You are good in soul, but a little harsh. The old man said to him: You are good but your soul is not tough.

Isidore of Pelusia said: Prize virtues, and do not care for worldly prosperity. For the former are certainly immortal, but the latter is so easily extinguished.

An old man said: Do not despise your neighbor, for you do not know whether the spirit of God is in you or in him. Well, I tell you, the one who serves you is your neighbor.

bba Epiphanus said: God sells righteousness very cheap to those who
are eager to buy: namely, for a little piece of
bread, worthless clothes, a cup of cold water
and one coin.

*A*bba Nilus said: Do not want things
to turn out as they seem best to you,
but as God pleases. Then you will be free of
confusion and thankful in your prayer.

*T*he brothers asked Abba Agathon: Father, which of the virtues of our way of life demands the greatest effort? He said to him: Forgive me, but there is no effort comparable to prayer to God. In fact, whenever you want to pray, hostile demons try to interrupt you. Of course they know that nothing but prayer to God entangles them. Certainly when you undertake any other good work, and persevere in it, you obtain rest. But prayer is a battle all the way to the last breath.

They asked Abba Macarius: How should we pray? The old man answered: A long speech is not necessary, but instead stretch out your hands and say, Lord, as you wish and as you know, have mercy. Yet if you feel a conflict is breaking out, you have to say, Lord, help! He knows what is good for us and treats us mercifully.

A brother asked Abba Matoes: What shall I do? My tongue causes me trouble and whenever I am among people, I cannot control it and I condemn them in all their good deeds and contradict them. What, therefore, shall I do? The old man answered him: If you cannot control yourself, go away from people and live alone. For this is a weakness. Those who live together with others ought not to be square, but

round, in order to turn toward all. Further, the old man said: I live alone not because of my virtue, but rather because of my weakness. You see, those who live among people are the strong ones.

*A*bba James said: We do not want words alone, for there are too many words among people today. What we need is action, for that is what we are looking for, not words which do not bear fruit.

EPILOGUE

Henri J.M. Nouwen

This text is drawn from unpublished lecture notes from a course on "Desert Spirituality & Contemporary Ministry," which Henri Nouwen taught at Yale Divinity School in 1980. It was this course, attended by Yushi Nomura, that inspired the creation of Desert Wisdom.—Eds. note

The spiritual life is the life of the Holy Spirit in us. The Holy Spirit is the spirit of Christ who leads us into the intimacy of the life between Father and Son. The Spirit makes us sons and daughters of God in the same full way as the Messiah was son.

This new life, this new identity, becomes visible in a new way of living, a new community, not based on competition but on a self-effacing ministry. The new mind, which is the mind of Jesus Christ, makes it possible to put the interests of others above our own.

To witness to this new life the early Christians were willing to give their lives. In fact martyrdom became *the* way to witness. But when the Church was no longer an enemy of society, a new form of martyrdom developed: the ascetical life in the desert.

The first aspect of desert spirituality is that it involves a leaving, a voluntary displacement. As Thomas Merton notes, the desert fathers regarded society as "a shipwreck from which each single individual person had to swim for his life. These were men and women who believed that to let oneself drift along, passively accepting the tenets and values of what they knew as society was purely and simply a disaster." The fact that the Emperor was now Christian and that "the world" was coming to know the Cross as a sign of temporal power only strengthened them in their resolve.

The so-called normal society was perceived by the desert fathers and mothers as a place that would make us drown. The only way to survive was to move away from the shipwreck and to find a place from which others could be saved. What is characteristic of the secular city is that it imprisons us in its *compulsions*. It is a life filled with *oughts* and *musts*. You *must* do this, you *ought* to do that, you *cannot* be here or there, and so forth. It is these compulsions which constitute the *false self*. The false self is the sense of self that is dependent on the response of the milieu. Who am I? I am the one who is liked, admired, respected, hated, and so forth.

"Compulsive" is indeed the best adjective for the false self. It points to the need for ongoing and increasing affirmation. This compulsiveness also leads to a very busy lifestyle. We have to keep up with all sorts of social obligations and we are constantly part of a balancing act in which we try to weigh very different social pressures, one against the other. This makes us very occupied and also preoccupied people.

What is important here is that we cannot simply get out of it by an act of the will. Often we find ourselves part of a complex system that does not tolerate any emptiness and space. There is—as Spinoza calls it—a *horror vacui*. It pulls us under. It forces us to participate. You cannot simply say, "Oh, I don't care what other people think of me. I do not let myself be affected by their praise or criticism." That is simply not possible. Our society is set up in such a way that you cannot survive unless you care. So what is asked for is a radical move, a voluntary displacement. This means moving from the ordinary and proper place in order to find our true self.

The second aspect of desert spirituality is the movement toward a different type of place—the move to the desert. The desert has two aspects: wilderness and paradise. On the one hand the desert is a dry and sterile place. It is the place of the demon. ("When the unclean spirit goes out of a person it wanders through waterless countries to look for a place to rest"—Luke 11:24.) The desert fathers are like paratroopers, people who go on the attack and unmask the enemy who hangs around the city. It is important to realize that when Jesus appears on the public scene the demons also appear. They are the first to recognize him and call him by his true name. Where God appears, the evil one is also present. In the city with its compulsions and compromises the lines between God and the demon have become blurred. Good is called evil and evil good. But in the desert the true struggle becomes clear. In the desert, where compulsions no longer rule us and we no longer can borrow an identity from the world, the question simply becomes: Are you for me or against me? Do you follow God or Mammon?

At the same time there is a wholly other side to the desert. The desert is also paradise. The desert life is the life by which we return to paradise. The monk does not just withdraw from the world, but is *en route* to paradise. God's grace will even make him find something of paradise here on earth as a consolation and comfort. Paradise means place of rapture, where things are heard that cannot be told (II Cor. 12:2). It is the celestial realm to which the Good Thief departed. It is a place of intimacy with the risen Christ. It is the state of paradise before the Fall. All these are assimilations of the Kingdom of God.

The best way to think of paradise is to think about it as a life in Christ. The desert fathers sought most of all their own true self in Christ. The proximate end of all their striving was "purity of heart," a clear unobstructed vision of the true state of affairs, an intuitive grasp of one's own inner reality as anchored—or rather lost—in God, through Christ. The fruit of this was "rest," the creation of inner space for God. A pure heart is a heart that is not attached to anything or anyone except God. A pure heart is a state of being single-minded, or perhaps "single-eyed."

Thus the desert is the fearful wilderness inhabited by the demons and the paradise where the first human being lived in harmony with God and creation. We find here the core reality of the spiritual life. The spiritual life is the life in which we come to see God, but also the demons.

I have often wondered why there is such an immense resistance in us to be with God. Why do we find prayer so hard, why do we always prefer to be busy instead of praying? Why do we keep seeing movies, going to parties, reading worthless books, running from one place to another? If God really exists and loves us, if he only wants to show us his love, why then is it so hard to give ourselves to him? Well, because when we enter into communion with God we have to face our demons, too. We have to face our greed, anger, lust, our rebellious nature, and our deep resentments against God himself. As long as we are busy and distracted we never really have to deal with who we are.

We cannot avoid going to the desert if we want to make God our only concern. The desert might mean very different things for different people but by simply staying in the murkiness and ambiguity of our daily lives we come to know neither God nor the demon and our lives remain absurd or blind. We never come to see reality as it really is and we build up an inner and outer world of illusions.

Paul went to the desert, and so did all great Christian leaders: Benedict, Francis, Martin Luther, John Wesley, George Fox, John Bunyan, Thomas Merton, Martin Luther King, Jr., Mother Teresa . . . They all broke out of the ordinary and proper life and went to face the demons. Demons can mean dying children on the streets of Calcutta, a nuclear arsenal that can destroy the world, hunger and other forms of oppression. But as soon as we start taking God seriously we will know who the enemy is.

Precisely because our resistance is so great we need disciplines. We need very concrete ways of living by which we can keep inner space open for God and grow into the new self. But as we struggle with the demons we will dis-cover that we are not struggling on our own but that it is the power of Christ himself who makes us victorious and it is that power that transforms us into new people. Indeed God re-makes us.

That is paradise: the new life in God.

AFTERWORD

Yushi Nomura

In the spring of 1978, thanks to a scholarship from the World Council of Churches, I found myself considering an opportunity to pursue studies at Yale Divinity School. On my first visit to the School, as I strolled through the corridors, I paused to look at the notice board full of fliers and posters.

As I stood there I sensed somebody approaching from the opposite end of the empty corridor. He stopped and stood right next to me. He seemed to be looking at me rather than the board. Feeling awkward, I returned his gaze, and found a middle-aged guy with uncombed, shaggy hair, dressed in an unironed shirt and a pretty well-seasoned windbreaker. I determined that he was probably a janitor. He grinned. I smiled back. "Hi, I'm Henry," he said. "What's your name?"

"I'm Yushi," I replied. "Nice to meet you, Henry." He grasped my hand and gave it an enthusiastic shake. "Nice meeting you here, Yushi," he said. Then he turned around and started to walk back the way he had come.

I liked this slightly odd but straightforward person. And suddenly my heart was filled with a warm feeling. Until a moment ago, this place had been totally foreign to me, but now I had a friend here, Henry the janitor. In fact it was this encounter with Henry the janitor that made me decide to join this community. His manner was a bit odd. But his attitude had conveyed the impression that he felt a bit lonely being left all alone on this campus during spring break, and, finding me standing here, he had wanted to make friends. I decided that when I returned I would seek him out and let him know that I was his friend and that I wouldn't let him feel alone.

In the fall, when I began my life as a student at Yale, I heard a good deal about the famous Professor Henri Nouwen. Arriving early for his class I noticed that all the seats were already taken and many students were standing along the walls. The only delightful surprise was to find my friend Henry there! Being the janitor it was evidently his job to clean the blackboard to get it ready for the lecture, and there he was, doing a very careful and meticulous job. He seemed to be taking his time, and I began to worry that he wouldn't finish before the bell rang. From the far end of the room I cheered him on in my heart: "Go, Henry, go! You better finish it quick, for the professor will appear any moment."

When he had finished cleaning the blackboard, Henry began to write a few words on the blackboard—strange words, like "anachoresis" and "hesychia." I was amazed that Henry wrote these words without reference to any notes. Some students had opened their notebooks and they began to write. Henry no longer looked like a janitor. "Who is he?" I asked a student beside me. "That is Professor Nouwen, of course," came the reply.

I later had occasion to remind Henri of our first meeting. He had no recollection of the incident, but he loved the honorable title of janitor so much that he asked me to repeat this story on many subsequent occasions. It was the beginning of our friendship.

In 1980, with Henri's guidance, I first encountered the spiritual realm of the desert mothers and fathers. Through his course on desert spirituality, I became familiar with those peculiar people who took flight into the desert in the fourth and fifth centuries as Christianity was being accepted by the Roman Empire. As I contemplated their stories I started to see them physically in my imagination. When I wrote a term paper for the course, I couldn't resist picking up my brush and ink and depicting them in the way I saw them. I attached this to my term paper, slightly fearful that the professor might see it as doodling, not suited to the serious subject matter. This worry was utterly dispelled by Henri's enthusiastic response. He encouraged me to display them in a small exhibition at Yale Divinity School and later he took them to his editor for the original edition of this book.

In the community life at YDS, Henri remained very close to the students and often he behaved as if he were just one of us. Whenever he was invited to students' gatherings and parties he would come by. And when he had to leave he would have trouble finding his coat for he often didn't remember what kind of coat he was wearing or whether he was wearing one at all. Or he would ask us questions such as, "Did I come by car? Was I driving? Do you know where I parked the car?"

On weekends we occasionally gathered at his apartment where we discussed everything from the problems of the world to personal questions like falling in love and healing broken hearts. Such evenings ended with a time of brief yet heartfelt prayer.

After one such gathering, when I volunteered to clean up the kitchen, I opened what I thought was a cupboard door only to find a very small altar with an icon beside it. In front of it was a small space, big enough for just one person. I closed the door immediately, feeling I had invaded someone's private space. Noticing this, Henri came and opened the door to show it to me in the manner of a little boy proudly showing off his secret hiding place.

"What is this place for?" I asked. "Oh, this is my personal prayer chapel," he answered. "I often meditate and pray in this place so that I can pray in solitude away from other people as Jesus told us to do." "But you live all by yourself here. You don't have to hide from other people."

To this Henri said, "When you want to pray seriously, you may have to stay away from yourself, you know."

As I was finishing this book I heard that Henri was planning to leave Yale. Could it be true? How sad and confusing for all of us. I had an image of one Abba, deciding to leave his community, one morning, to get deeper into the desert, seeking to get even closer to the spirit of Jesus.

A few days after an extravagent farewell party for Henri, I received a peculiar call from him. He sounded tense and desperate. "Are you there, Yushi? Do you remember me?" I went straight to the house where he was staying, where I found him standing wordlessly. Over a cup of tea he started to talk. "I had a terrible daydream. A lot of good friends gathered and started to dance around me. When the music stopped and the dust settled, there was nobody left. I found myself in the middle of a barren land." "You're not alone, Henri," I said. "You know we've been working together in that desert." "I know, I know. Thank you for reminding me that I'm in the middle of the desert and I'm not alone there."

When one goes into the deepest part of the human soul, one cannot ask someone to accompany him. Step by step, he has to go down all the way to the bottom. When he finds something shining there, he holds it to his bosom, and starts going up the way he came down so that he can share it with others.

In 1996 a heart attack claimed his life. Henri took off to a higher place much earlier than any of us could have possibly imagined. A few months before he left us, he took the initiative to contact me to work on this book again together. I have a feeling that his idea was to draw the spirits of the Abbas and Ammas into today's world where they are much needed. Although there is no way to know what kind of shape it would have taken, I am very glad that this book has been given a second chance to be put under a reading light, thanks to Robert Ellsberg and the other wonderful people at Orbis.

As the new century of our Lord has just started, the entire human civilization seems to be facing something similar to what the ancient Roman Empire experienced right before it started to fall. It was the time of history when our Abbas and Ammas took flight into the desert to seek and to live in the spirit of Jesus. Following the fall of the Empire, a new era, the Medieval Age, started. The foundation of this new era was prepared and sustained by the monastic movement which had its origin in the faith and lifestyle of the desert fathers and mothers described in this book. I am convinced that their spirit in Jesus would guide us today through the desert where we find ourselves, and lead us into the new era of our Lord.

Tokyo, January 1, 2001